AMAZING INVENTORY OF INCREDIBLE KNOWLEDGE

PUB TIME

USELESS TRIVIA

Publications International, Ltd.

Contributing Writer: Holli Fort

Cover Photo: Shutterstock.com

Louis Weber, CEO
Publications International, Ltd.
7373 North Cicero Avenue
Lincolnwood, Illinois 60712

ISBN-13: 978-1-4508-7826-5
ISBN-10: 1-4508-7826-1

Manufactured in Canada

8 7 6 5 4 3 2 1

CONTENTS

TRIVIA TIME

Welcome to *Pub Time Useless Trivia*. This is not your typical trivia book. If you're looking for dry and dusty trivia, you won't find it here. But if you think you know—or want to know—what European capital has more dogs than people, how ancient Romans whitened their teeth, or which Pez dispenser is most rare, look no further. Here you'll discover where the world's saltiest body of water is located, how many quills the average porcupine has, and many other utterly useless trivia facts.

Pub Time Useless Trivia is organized into categories, making it easy for you to "pick your poison," so to speak. This collection delves into the kind of factoids that will stump even the most fanatical trivia buffs. You'll find questions on the right-hand pages and answers on the left-hand pages.

Are you ready to put your trivia know-how to the test? Grab a chair, pull out *Pub Time Useless Trivia*, and get ready for an entertaining night.

AMERICANA

1. IN WHICH SOUTHERN STATE CAN YOU FIND THE TOWNS REPUBLICAN AND DEMOCRAT?

A. North Carolina

B. Georgia

C. South Carolina

D. Arkansas

2. THIS'LL PERK YOU RIGHT UP! WHICH OF THESE IS *NOT* A REAL TOWN NAMED AFTER AMERICA'S FAVORITE CAFFEINATED BEVERAGE?

A. Hot Coffee, Mississippi

B. Coffeeville, Alabama

C. Coffee Creek, Montana

D. Coffee Cup, Washington

1.

A. Though each party is known for digging in its Tar Heels when debate season rolls around.

2.

D. But it's a sponsorship opportunity for Starbucks!

3. WHICH STATE IS HOME TO THE ONLY ACTIVE DIAMOND MINE IN THE UNITED STATES?

A. Montana

B. Arkansas

C. West Virginia

D. Oklahoma

4. THE UNITED STATES HAS NEVER LOST A WAR IN WHICH WHAT WERE USED?

A. Torpedoes

B. Horses and bayonets

C. Cannons

D. Mules

5. IN WHICH HAND DOES THE STATUE OF LIBERTY HOLD A TORCH?

3.

B. At Crater of Diamonds State Park, it's finders keepers (after a small entry fee, naturally). Can you dig it?

4.

D. Presumably the mules were just too stubborn to give up.

5.

Right. In the statue's left hand is a tablet inscribed with the date July IV MDCCLXXVI—July 4, 1776—to commemorate American independence.

6. WHICH ANIMAL-NAMED CITY IS THE COW-CHIP-THROWING CAPITAL OF THE WORLD?

A. Buffalo, New York

B. Beaver, Oklahoma

C. Porcupine, South Dakota

D. Alligator, Mississippi

7. WHICH WOMAN IS THE SUBJECT OF THE MOST AMERICAN STATUES?

A. Sacagawea

B. Sojourner Truth

C. Annie Oakley

D. Amelia Earhart

8. WHICH OF THESE "ALPHABET AGENCIES" WAS *NOT* PART OF THE NEW DEAL?

A. CCC

B. FDIC

C. SEC

D. CDC

6.

B. BYOC (Bring Your Own Chips) for this can't-miss competition each April.

7.

A. And if you need to settle a dispute, you can always flip a golden Sacagawea dollar.

8.

D. The Centers for Disease Control and Prevention (CDC) was established in 1946, about 10 years after the Great Depression and the start of the New Deal agencies. The Civilian Conservation Corps (CCC), Federal Deposit Insurance Corporation (FDIC), and Securities Exchange Commission (SEC) were part of the New Deal.

9. THE PROUD AMERICAN MOTTO "E PLURIBUS UNUM"—OUT OF MANY, ONE— WAS ORIGINALLY USED BY THE ANCIENT ROMAN POET VIRGIL TO DESCRIBE WHAT FOODSTUFF?

A. Lasagna

B. Salad dressing

C. Pizza

D. Dessert wine

10. HOW MANY SPIKES ARE THERE IN THE STATUE OF LIBERTY'S CROWN?

11. WHAT IS PRESIDENT BARACK OBAMA'S SECRET SERVICE CODE NAME?

A. Rogue

B. Renegade

C. Rambo

D. Rascal

11

9.

B. No word on whether Virgil preferred oil and vinegar over ranch.

10.

Seven, symbolizing the seven seas.

11.

B. The whole Obama family has "R" code names: Michelle is Renaissance, while daughters Malia and Sasha are Radiance and Rosebud, respectively.

12. IN WHAT MAJOR CITY CAN YOU FIND THE MAGNIFICENT MILE?

A. Chicago

B. New Orleans

C. Seattle

D. New York

13. BEFORE IT WAS SETTLED IN WASHINGTON, D.C., THE U.S. CAPITAL WAS IN EIGHT OTHER CITIES. WHICH OF THESE DID *NOT* SERVE AS THE CAPITAL?

A. Philadelphia, Pennsylvania

B. Montpelier, Vermont

C. Trenton, New Jersey

D. Baltimore, Maryland

14. TRUE OR FALSE?

Hugh Hefner saved the famous Hollywood sign by hosting a fund-raiser at the Playboy Mansion.

13

12.

A. This famous shopping destination sprawls along Michigan Avenue in the Windy City.

13.

B. Montpelier, Vermont did not serve as the U.S. capital. Lancaster, Pennsylvania; York, Pennsylvania; Princeton, New Jersey; Annapolis, Maryland; and Manhattan, New York also took turns as the nation's capital.

14.

True. Hefner offered stars the chance to "adopt" the letters of the sign for $27,500 each, and started things off by adopting the Y himself. Actor Gene Autry bought an L. Rocker Alice Cooper saved an O. The rebuilt sign was unveiled in November 1978.

15. TRUE OR FALSE?

At least one early president was a big fan of skinny-dipping.

16. COLONEL SANDERS (OF KFC FAME) WAS NAMED AN HONORARY KENTUCKY COLONEL BY THE STATE'S GOVERNOR, AND HE'S IN GOOD COMPANY. WHICH OF THESE FIGURES WAS *NOT* MADE AN HONORARY KENTUCKY COLONEL?

A. Muhammad Ali

B. Pope John Paul II

C. Al Gore

D. Whoopi Goldberg

17. CONNECTICUT WAS THE FIRST STATE TO SET A SPEED LIMIT. AT WHAT "BLAZING" SPEED WOULD CARS HIT THAT LIMIT?

A. 5 miles per hour

B. 7 miles per hour

C. 9 miles per hour

D. 12 miles per hour

15.

True: John Quincy Adams started each summer day with a swim au naturel in the Potomac River.

16.

C. It's hard to imagine this group sitting on the veranda drinking mint juleps together.

17.

D. Outside of city limits, however, cars could travel at the breakneck pace of 15 miles per hour.

18. WHAT IS THE OFFICIAL STATE SPORT OF MARYLAND?

A. Jousting

B. Shuffleboard

C. Dressage

D. Sailing

19. WE'RE USED TO SEEING PORTRAITS OF GEORGE WASHINGTON WITH A POWDERED WIG. WHAT COLOR WAS HIS HAIR UNDERNEATH IT?

A. Blonde

B. Brown

C. Black

D. Red

20. HAWAII HAS EIGHT MAJOR ISLANDS. HOW MANY CAN YOU NAME?

18.

A. No word on whether Medieval Times is the official restaurant, though.

19.

D. Washington was a carrot-top! Thomas Jefferson and Martin Van Buren round out the presidential redhead contingent.

20.

Hawaii (the Big Island), Kahoolawe, Kauai, Lanai, Maui, Molokai, Niihau, and Oahu

1. TWO-TIME *PEOPLE* SEXIEST MAN ALIVE GEORGE CLOONEY HAD A CLOSE AND LASTING RELATIONSHIP WITH WHAT ANIMAL UNTIL ITS DEATH IN 2006?

   A. Jersey, a hedgehog

   B. Max, a potbellied pig

   C. Edgar, a bearded dragon lizard

   D. Frank, a ferret

2. WHICH OF THESE ANIMALS HAS THE LOUDEST CALL?

   A. Elephant

   B. Howler monkey

   C. Blue whale

   D. African lion

1.

B. Clooney's committed relationship with Max lasted 18 years—a very long time indeed for this confirmed bachelor.

2.

C. The call of the blue whale registers an incredible 188 decibels, making it the loudest animal on Earth. Hey, if you had to search the entire ocean for a mate, you'd speak up too!

3. KEEPING UP WITH THE PRESIDENT IS A JOB THAT'S FOR THE DOGS! CAN YOU MATCH THESE RECENT COMMANDERS IN CHIEF WITH THEIR CANINE COMPANIONS?

1. Barack Obama

2. George W. Bush

3. Bill Clinton

4. George H. W. Bush

A. Buddy

B. Barney

C. Millie

D. Bo

4. ABOUT 20 TIMES A DAY IN THE UNITED STATES, BIRDS AND AIRPLANES COLLIDE. WHAT'S THE INDUSTRY TERM FOR THE GOOEY AFTERMATH OF SUCH A CRASH?

A. Ploogie

B. Nardle

C. Malpom

D. Snarge

3.

1. D; 2. B; 3. A; 4. C.

4.

D. Snarge is no joke! The U.S. Air Force alone spends about $60 million per year repairing damage caused by close encounters of the winged kind.

5. HOW MANY DIFFERENT DOGS PLAYED THE TITLE ROLE OF THE TELEVISION SHOW *LASSIE*?

6. WHICH OF THE FOLLOWING IS *NOT* A POISONOUS SNAKE?

A. Viper

B. Viperine

C. Eastern Brown Snake

D. Black Mamba

7. MANY KINDS OF CATERPILLARS HAVE EVOLVED TO DEVELOP A UNIQUE CAMOUFLAGE. WHAT MATERIAL DO THEIR BODIES EMULATE?

A. Leaves

B. Roadside litter

C. Tree bark

D. Bird droppings

8. TRUE OR FALSE?

Opossums mate through the female's nostrils.

5.

In its 20-year run, nine different collies helped extricate Timmy and other kids from perilous situations involving bodies of water, cliffs, quicksand, and mine shafts—though never from a well.

6.

B. Viperines aren't poisonous snakes, but they play them on TV...or, you know, in the wild. When in danger, these harmless snakes ward off enemies by flattening their heads into a triangle shape that mimics those of their more venomous brethren.

7.

D. Sometimes the best defense is a really compelling argument: "Don't eat me, I taste like poo!"

8.

False. Opossums mate in a normal way; if by "normal" you mean that the male has a forked (bifid) penis. Luckily for opossum kind, the female has two uteri, which works out well for them both.

9. WHICH ANIMAL HAS A BRAIN SMALLER THAN EITHER OF ITS EYEBALLS?

A. Owl

B. Ostrich

C. Turkey

D. Eagle

10. WHICH ANIMALS ARE MOST FREQUENTLY "HONORED" AS MASCOTS AT FOUR-YEAR COLLEGES?

A. Cougars

B. Bears

C. Bulldogs

D. Eagles

11. WHAT BACK-FROM-THE-BRINK-OF-EXTINCTION SPECIES IS NICKNAMED THE "PIG WHISTLE"?

A. Javan rhino

B. Northern hairy-nosed wombat

C. Vancouver Island marmot

D. Dwarf blue sheep

9.

B. Ostriches are super-fast (they can run up to 45 miles per hour!) but their small brain size may explain why they are still an easy target for predators: They tend to run in circles.

10.

D. With 74 teams bearing it as a symbol, the eagle soars to victory. Bulldogs rank third with 39, bears seventh with 30, and cougars ninth with 27.

11.

C. Vancouver Island marmots have five distinct whistles, but the one that earned them their nickname is a loud, piercing whistle that sounds the alarm for a nearby predator.

12. HOW MANY QUILLS DOES THE AVERAGE PORCUPINE HAVE?

A. 30,000

B. 40,000

C. 50,000

D. 80,000

13. WHICH OF THESE ANIMALS HAS ONLY ONE STOMACH?

A. Goat

B. Deer

C. Moose

D. Horse

14. A MATURE EWE YIELDS BETWEEN 7 AND 10 POUNDS OF SHORN WOOL PER YEAR. THIS IS, COINCIDENTALLY, THE AMOUNT NEEDED TO DO WHAT?

A. Line a pair of Uggs

B. Make a man's suit

C. Weave an area rug

D. Cover the playing surface of a pool table

12.

A. And each is a sharp reminder that if you poke at a porcupine, it will poke you back!

13.

D. The others are ruminants, animals with four digestive chambers.

14.

B. But when it comes to the choice of necktie, bowtie, or cravat, you'll have to suit yourself.

15. DO FISH SLEEP?

16. WHERE DID THE MANX CAT ORIGINATE?

A. Hawaii

B. Australia

C. Isle of Man

D. Cuba

17. TRUE OR FALSE?

Giraffes are the mammals with the lowest blood pressure.

18. HOW IS THE GENDER OF AN ALLIGATOR DETERMINED?

A. Chromosomes from the mother

B. Chromosomes from the father

C. Temperature during incubation

D. Timing of fertilization related to tide chart

15.

Not the way we do—the whole "having no eyelids" thing puts a damper on that. Mostly fish rest in a state akin to daydreaming. They just ... drift along.

16

C. The Manx's lack of tail is caused by a gene mutation—which sure puts those Teenage Mutant Ninja Turtles to shame!

17.

False. Giraffes have blood pressure that is twice as high as other animals. It takes a lot of pumping for blood to reach a giraffe's head! Luckily, giraffes have small but shockingly strong hearts that are up for the job.

18.

C. Alligators lack chromosomes for sex determination. Hot temperatures during incubation produce males, while cooler temperatures produce females.

19. WHICH OF THESE BIG CATS CANNOT ROAR?

A. Lions

B. Tigers

C. Leopards

D. Cheetahs

20. TRUE OR FALSE?

Shark embryos use their sharp teeth to kill each other in the womb in a sort of embryonic cage match.

19.

D. Cheetahs have more in common with their domesticated small cousins—while they can't roar, they can purr while inhaling and exhaling.

20.

True. Shark fetuses will kill and eat other fetuses by the score in order to increase their chances of making it to birth.

ART & LITERATURE

1. WHAT BOOK IS THE VOLUME MOST COMMONLY STOLEN FROM LIBRARIES AROUND THE WORLD?

A. Merriam-Webster's Dictionary

B. *Joy of Cooking*

C. *Guinness Book of World Records*

D. *Roget's Thesaurus*

2. WHICH CHARLES DICKENS NOVEL WAS ORIGINALLY GIVEN THE "GUARANTEED INSTANT CLASSIC" TITLE *TOM-ALL-ALONE'S FACTORY THAT GOT INTO CHANCERY AND NEVER GOT OUT*?

A. *Bleak House*

B. *Great Expectations*

C. *A Christmas Carol*

D. *The Pickwick Papers*

1.

C. The record holder holds a record. The Bible is the volume most commonly stolen from stores.

2.

A. With the original title, the book's sales numbers would have been *Bleak* indeed.

3. WHICH WELL-KNOWN WRITER COINED THE WORD "NERD"?

A. Roald Dahl

B. Lewis Carroll

C. Dr. Seuss

D. J.R.R. Tolkien

4. WHAT BOOK DOES NOT CONTAIN A SINGLE LETTER "E"?

A. *Gadsby* by Ernest Wright

B. *To Kill a Mockingbird* by Harper Lee

C. *Catch-22* by Joseph Heller

D. *Lolita* by Vladimir Nabokov

5. WHICH IS *NOT* THE FIRST LINE OF A FAMOUS NOVEL?

A. "Marley was dead, to begin with. There is no doubt whatever about that."

B. "Anderson had enjoyed ten years of being totally irresponsible."

C. "When he was nearly thirteen, my brother Jem got his arm badly broken at the elbow."

D. "It was a pleasure to burn."

3.

C. Prescient as always, Seuss portrayed his nerd with rumpled hair and a black t-shirt in the 1950 book *If I Ran the Zoo*.

4.

A. The 1939 book's subtitle offers a helpful hint: *A Story of Over 50,000 Words Without Using the Letter "E."*

5.

B. The others are from Charles Dickens's *A Christmas Carol*, Harper Lee's *To Kill a Mockingbird*, and Ray Bradbury's *Fahrenheit 451*.

6. **WHICH OPERA TELLS THE STORY OF A NOBLEMAN WITH AN EYE FOR THE LADIES WHO IS ULTIMATELY PUNISHED BY BEING SENT TO HELL?**

A. *Tosca*

B. *La Traviata*

C. *Don Giovanni*

D. *La Bohème*

7. **WHO IS *NOT* ONE OF THE BRONTË SISTERS?**

A. Anne

B. Charlotte

C. Emily

D. Elizabeth

8. **VINCENT VAN GOGH SOLD ONLY ONE PAINTING DURING HIS LIFETIME. WHAT WAS IT?**

A. *The Red Vineyard*

B. *Starry Night*

C. *Blossoming Almond Tree*

D. *The Night Café*

6.

C. Mozart's hero is better known by the translation of his name, Don Juan.

7.

D. Each sister was a famous novelist in her own right, but they "burst" onto the literary scene together with a book of poetry under the pen names Currer, Ellis, and Acton Bell—and the book sold a whopping two copies.

8.

A. The work sold for a mere 400 francs a few months before the painter's death—a far cry from the $82.5 million his *Portrait of Doctor Gachet* sold for in 1990.

9. **IF YOU TAKE A TRIP TO THE CAPITOL WITH EFFIE TRINKET, WHERE ARE YOU LIKELY TO BE GOING?**

A. Panem

B. Oz

C. Middle-Earth

D. Narnia

10. **WHAT IS THE BEST-SELLING LITTLE GOLDEN BOOK OF ALL TIME?**

A. *The Poky Little Puppy*

B. *The Little Red Hen*

C. *This Little Piggy*

D. *Three Little Kittens*

11. **IN THE BOOK SERIES *PERCY JACKSON AND THE OLYMPIANS*, CAMP HALF-BLOOD IS A PLACE THAT WELCOMES WHAT?**

A. Mythological monsters

B. Demigods

C. Humans

D. The dead

9.

A. You are likely to be headed into the Arena with the other tributes in Suzanne Collins's best-selling *Hunger Games* trilogy. But be careful: Twenty-four tributes enter, but only one can leave!

10.

A. More than 15 million copies of this classic book have sold since it was published in September 1942.

11.

B. Percy Jackson and fellow campers are demigods —having one human and one god for parents.

12. THE LATE 1970s TV SHOW *SHIELDS AND YARNELL* WAS A SHOWCASE FOR WHAT PERFORMANCE ART?

A. Break dance

B. Sculpture

C. Mime

D. Yarn bombing

13. WHICH WRITER WAS COMMISSIONED BY PRESIDENT BILL CLINTON TO WRITE A POEM FOR HIS 1993 INAUGURATION?

A. Maya Angelou

B. Gwendolyn Brooks

C. Rita Dove

D. Louise Gluck

14. WHICH ARTIST PAINTED *THE PERSISTENCE OF MEMORY*, A SURREALIST WORK FEATURING MELTING TIMEPIECES?

A. Vincent van Gogh

B. Salvador Dalí

C. Frida Kahlo

D. Paul Gauguin

12.

C. Mimes Robert Shields and Lorene Yarnell were married in a mime wedding in Union Square and went on to win an Emmy for their television program.

13.

A. Angelou wrote "On the Pulse of the Morning" for the occasion.

14.

B. And college dorm room walls all over the world are thankful for it!

15. **EARLY COMIC BOOK ARTISTS TOOK INSPIRATION FOR SUPERHEROES' TIGHTS AND CAPES FROM WHAT PROFESSION?**

A. Professional wrestlers

B. Ballet dancers

C. Competitive swimmers

D. Kings

16. **WHICH CLASSIC DUTCH PAINTER CHOSE HIMSELF AS ONE OF HIS FAVORITE SUBJECTS?**

A. Johannes Vermeer

B. Frans Hals

C. Rembrandt van Rijn

D. Jan de Bray

17. **WHO AUTHORED THE FIRST NOVEL WRITTEN ON A TYPEWRITER?**

A. Mark Twain

B. Harriet Beecher Stowe

C. Louisa May Alcott

D. Jack London

15.

A. Professional wrestlers and circus strongmen in the early twentieth century needed tight outfits for maximum flexibility and visual appeal. The briefs-over-tights look popularized by superheroes was born from necessity: Since Lycra and elastic weren't yet invented, there was a good chance performers could split their tights. As insurance against exposing their "little performers" to the world, they wore trunks over their tights.

16.

C. Rembrandt produced around 70 self-portraits—that's a lot of mirror gazing!

17.

A. Although there is some debate over exactly which book it was (*The Adventures of Tom Sawyer*, as Twain recalled, or *Life on the Mississippi*, as most scholars agree), Twain wrote in a 1904 letter, "I will now claim—until dispossessed—that I was the first person in the world to apply the type-machine to literature."

18. ON WHICH CELESTIAL BODY CAN YOU FIND THE MONA LISA CRATER, NAMED FOR THE PAINTING BY LEONARDO DA VINCI?

A. The moon

B. Mercury

C. Venus

D. Mars

19. WHICH PHOTOGRAPHER IS RENOWNED FOR BLACK AND WHITE PORTRAITS OF NATURAL SETTINGS?

A. Dorothea Lange

B. Annie Liebovitz

C. Henri Cartier-Bresson

D. Ansel Adams

20. A CEPHALOPHORE IS AN ARTISTIC DEPICTION OF A SAINT HOLDING WHAT?

A. Cat

B. Bible

C. Head

D. Cross

18.

C. In keeping with the planet's name (Venus was the goddess of love), its craters are all named for women.

19.

D. Adams's photos are particularly important to environmentalists, as they celebrate the beauty of nature and were often featured in Sierra Club publications.

20.

C. The saint carries his or her own head as a symbol of having been martyred—which makes halo placement tricky indeed.

BODY

1. A LAUGH EXPELS AIR OUT OF THE BODY AT SPEEDS UP TO **70** MILES PER HOUR. WHAT IS THE SPEED OF THE AIR RELEASED WITH A SNEEZE?

A. 80 miles per hour

B. 100 miles per hour

C. 120 miles per hour

D. 140 miles per hour

2. IF YOU ACCIDENTALLY KNOCK OUT A TOOTH, IN WHAT LIQUID SHOULD YOU STORE IT TO IMPROVE THE CHANCES OF THE DENTIST BEING ABLE TO RE-IMPLANT IT?

A. Beer (preferably stout)

B. Water

C. Juice

D. Milk

1.

B. The sneeze is a powerful weapon—it can send 100,000 germs into the air in a single speedy bound!

2.

D. The proteins and antibacterial properties of milk keep the cells alive—definitely doing the body good.

3. CAN A HAIR TEST SHOW IF YOU SMOKED MARIJUANA?

4. TRUE OR FALSE?

Each of your nostrils registers smell differently.

5. WHAT DOES THE "LITTLE BROTHER CURE" FOR HICCUPS INVOLVE?

A. Crossing your eyes

B. Pulling the sides of your mouth outward with both index fingers

C. Mimicking each word said by someone older than you

D. Sticking out your tongue

6. IN WHAT PART OF THE BODY CAN YOU FIND THE ONLY BONE THAT IS NOT CONNECTED TO ANY OTHER BONES?

A. Wrist

B. Lungs

C. Throat

D. Pelvis

QUESTIONS

3.

Hair can be tested for the presence of marijuana, but the test can't tell if you personally smoked the weed or if your hair just absorbed the chemicals from that last Phish show you went to. A urine or blood test is needed to verify that.

4.

True. The right nostril detects the more pleasant smells, but the left one...is more accurate.

5.

D. This stimulates the glottis, the opening of the airway to the lungs. Since a closed glottis is the usual cause of hiccups, this treatment generally works.

6.

C. The hyoid bone, which helps support the tongue when talking, is connected only by ligaments.

7. WHAT PART OF YOUR BODY WOULD YOU USE FOR GURNING?

A. Hands

B. Abs

C. Face

D. Shoulders

8. WHAT IS THE LARGEST MUSCLE IN THE BODY?

A. Pectoralis major

B. Gluteus maximus

C. Adductor longus

D. Gastrocnemius

9. WILL COFFEE SOBER YOU UP?

10. WHICH OF THESE TECHNIQUES COULD *NOT* BE USED TO IDENTIFY A SPECIFIC PERSON?

A. Eye scan

B. Tongue print

C. Nose print

D. Fingerprint

7.

C. Gurning is a contest in which professionals compete to see who can pull the "world's ugliest face." Those who practice enough might make it to the Egremont Gurning Championship, held every September in Cumbria, England.

8.

B. All that junk is there to support your trunk.

9

No amount of coffee, soda, water, or anything other than time will do the trick. So if you've been drinking, spend your money on a cab rather than a cappuccino.

10.

C. Nose printing can be used to identify pets and livestock, but humans mostly just leave indistinct smudges.

11. WHICH ITEM IS RESPONSIBLE FOR MOST CASES OF CHOKING IN THE UNITED STATES?

A. Pen/pencil

B. Toothpick

C. Peanut

D. Carrot

12. WHAT IS THE MOST COMMON PLASTIC SURGERY IN AMERICA?

A. Nose job

B. Breast augmentation

C. Liposuction

D. Face-lift

13. HOW LONG DOES IT TAKE FOR FOOD TO TRAVEL FROM THE MOUTH TO THE STOMACH?

A. 7 seconds

B. 32 seconds

C. 1 minute

D. 3 minutes

11.

B. Maybe stick to floss next time...

12.

C. Be prepared: Getting the fat sucked out of your abdomen, buttocks, hips, thighs, or upper arms will suck about $2,300 out of your wallet.

13.

B. And it doesn't take much longer from the lips to the hips!

14. TRUE OR FALSE?

Fingernails and toenails grow at the same speed.

15. WHAT DO THE CONES IN THE EYES HELP YOU DO?

A. See at greater distances

B. See in color

C. See nearby objects

D. See in black and white

16. WHICH LUNG IS LARGER THAN THE OTHER?

17. HOW MANY DIFFERENT SHADES OF THE COLOR GRAY CAN THE HUMAN EYE DISTINGUISH?

18. WHAT WAS THE FIRST HUMAN ORGAN TO BE SUCCESSFULLY TRANSPLANTED?

A. Lung

B. Kidney

C. Heart

D. Liver

14.

False. Fingernails grow two to three times faster than toenails.

15.

B. Each eye has 6 to 7 million cones to help you find just the right shade of blue.

16.

The right—the left has to accommodate the heart.

17.

50 Shades of Grey? Bah. Eyes can detect about 500 different shades of the color.

18.

B. The first successful transplant took place in 1954 in Boston. Since the surgery predated the discovery of anti-rejection drugs, it was a good thing the patients were identical twins so the organ was not rejected.

19. IN WHICH FIELD OF MEDICINE IS
AMNIOCENTESIS USED?

A. Obstetrics

B. Cardiology

C. Orthopedics

D. Urology

20. WHICH FAMOUS ACTOR IS A GREAT
EXAMPLE OF HETEROCHROMIA?

A. Tom Cruise

B. Julia Roberts

C. Tom Hanks

D. Jane Seymour

19.

A. This test screens for potential problems with a fetus—and can tell gender.

20.

D. Seymour has eyes that are two different colors: one is brown and the other is green.

1. **KOKOMO, INDIANA, IS KNOWN AS THE "CITY OF FIRSTS." WHICH OF THESE PRODUCTS WAS *NOT* A FIRST FOR KOKOMO?**

A. Mechanical corn picker

B. Stainless steel

C. Computer

D. Push-button car radio

2. **WHICH CITY WAS THE FIRST TO OPEN A BRANCH OF THE U.S. STOCK EXCHANGE?**

A. New York

B. Philadelphia

C. Washington, D.C.

D. Boston

1.

C. The world's first computer was developed at the University of Pennsylvania.

2.

B. It opened in 1790, ironically enough, at the London Coffee House.

3. **WHAT WAS THE FIRST TOY TO BE FEATURED IN A TELEVISION COMMERCIAL?**

A. Easy-Bake Oven

B. Barbie

C. Mr. Potato Head

D. Hula Hoop

4. **THE FIRST WORDS SPOKEN ON THE TELEPHONE WERE "MR. WATSON, COME HERE; I WANT YOU." WHAT WERE THE CONTENTS OF THE FIRST TELEGRAM?**

5. **TRUE OR FALSE?**

The Barbie doll first appeared in an astronaut uniform to commemorate Sally Ride's 1983 space shuttle mission, the first undertaken by an American woman.

6. **WHAT WAS THE NICKNAME GIVEN TO THE FIRST TV REMOTE CONTROL?**

A. Lazy Bones

B. Spud

C. Barcalounger

D. Idle Hands

3.

C. And the advertising paid off—the spud made more than $4 million in sales for Hasbro in just its first few months.

4.

"What hath God wrought!" read the telegram from Samuel Morse on May 24, 1844.

5.

False. Barbie got her astronaut on in 1965, nearly 20 years before Ride. Was it prescience—or optimism?

6.

A. Couch potatoes everywhere rejoiced when the remote finally went public in 1956.

7. WHAT WAS ROCK MUSIC'S FIRST "SUPERGROUP"—A MUSICAL ACT IN WHICH ALL OF THE MEMBERS HAD ALREADY HAD SUCCESSFUL CAREERS AS PART OF A BAND OR SOLO ACT?

A. Cream

B. Crosby, Stills & Nash

C. Emerson, Lake & Palmer

D. Traveling Wilburys

8. WHAT WAS THE MAIN COURSE OF THE FIRST TV DINNER?

A. Salisbury steak

B. Turkey

C. Fried chicken

D. Macaroni and cheese

9. WHAT WAS THE FIRST AMERICAN DAILY COMIC STRIP?

A. *The Katzenjammer Kids*

B. *Happy Hooligan*

C. *A. Piker Clerk*

D. *The Yellow Kid*

63

7.

A. Eric Clapton, Jack Bruce, and Ginger Baker were stars in their own right before they formed Cream, which released its first album in 1967. Unfortunately, the relationship soured in only two years.

8.

B. Swanson had 260 tons of leftover frozen turkey after Thanksgiving 1953, and found a clever way to turn disaster into profit: load portions of turkey, peas, sweet potatoes, and cornbread dressing onto an aluminum tray, and voila! A portable feast was born.

9.

C. The strip by Clare Briggs first appeared in the *Chicago American* in 1904.

10. THE FIRST PIZZERIA IN THE WORLD OPENED IN NAPLES, ITALY, IN 1738. WHAT WAS IT CALLED?

A. Atza Pizzeria

B. Angelo's Pizzeria

C. Antica Pizzeria

D. Aberto Pizzeria

11. WHO WAS THE FIRST WOMAN TO SERVE ON THE U.S. SUPREME COURT?

A. Ruth Bader Ginsburg

B. Sonia Sotomayor

C. Elena Kagan

D. Sandra Day O'Connor

12. DOLLY, THE FIRST SUCCESSFULLY CLONED MAMMAL, WAS WHAT KIND OF ANIMAL?

A. Cow

B. Pig

C. Sheep

D. Chicken

10.

C. The pizzeria features ovens lined with volcanic rock from Mount Vesuvius, and it's still in business today if you are in the neighborhood and want an "authentic" slice.

11.

D. Justice O'Connor was nominated by president Reagan in 1981 and served until 2006.

12.

C. Dolly the sheep lived only six years, 1996–2003. Her taxidermied remains, however, live on at the National Museum of Scotland.

13. THE FIRST AOL INSTANT MESSAGE WAS SENT JANUARY 6, 1993, FROM TED LEONSIS TO HIS WIFE. THE IM SAID: "DON'T BE SCARED...IT IS ME. LOVE YOU AND MISS YOU." WHAT WAS HER REPLY?

A. "LOL!"

B. No reply (she didn't understand how IM worked)

C. "Love you too."

D. "Wow...this is so cool!"

14. WHICH ACTRESS WAS THE FIRST *PLAYBOY* CENTERFOLD?

A. Marilyn Monroe

B. Jayne Mansfield

C. Bettie Page

D. Barbara Windsor

15. WHO WAS THE FIRST WOMAN IN SPACE?

A. Sally Ride

B. Svetlana Savitskaya

C. Eileen Collins

D. Valentina Tereshkova

13.

D. No word on whether either punctuated their messages with emoticons.

14.

A. Monroe didn't pose specifically for the men's magazine; publisher Hugh Hefner purchased a nude photo of the actress from another source for his inaugural 1953 issue.

15.

D. Tereshkova took a space ride June 16, 1963—a full 20 years before Ride became the first American woman to duplicate the feat.

16. **Elizabeth Taylor was famously married eight times. Which of these husbands was her first?**

A. Richard Burton

B. Conrad Hilton

C. Michael Todd

D. Larry Fortensky

17. **The first parachutist was a brave soul who plunged 3,200 feet down to what city?**

A. Paris

B. London

C. Rome

D. St. Petersburg

18. **What car make did Ray Harroun drive to victory in 1911 in the first Indianapolis 500?**

A. Mercedes

B. Marmon

C. Mercer

D. McFarlan

16.

B. The hotel heir (and great-uncle to Paris and Nicky!) was married to the actress for less than a year when she was 18.

17.

A. André-Jacques Garnerin jumped from a hydrogen balloon floating above the City of Lights on October 22, 1797.

18.

B. Harroun took home a whopping $14,250 prize for winning the inaugural race.

19. **THE FIRST NUCLEAR EXPLOSION TOOK PLACE IN 1945 IN NEW MEXICO. WHAT WAS THE NAME OF THE TEST PROJECT?**

A. Unity

B. Trinity

C. Divinity

D. Complicity

20. **PARK-O-METER NO. 1, THE WORLD'S FIRST PARKING METER, WAS INSTALLED IN 1935 AT THE CORNER OF FIRST STREET AND ROBINSON AVENUE IN WHAT CITY?**

A. New York City

B. Kansas City

C. Oklahoma City

D. Atlantic City

19.

B. Trinity took place, appropriately enough, in the Jornada del Muerto (Journey of Death) desert.

20.

B. Less than a month later, the first parking ticket was given—to a guy who swore he was just running into a store to get change for the meter. (He was a reverend, so we're inclined to believe him.)

FOOD & DRINK

1. UNTIL THE NINETEENTH CENTURY, MOST AMERICANS BELIEVED THAT THE "LOVE APPLE" (TOMATO) WAS WHAT?

A. A vegetable

B. Poisonous

C. The original apple from the Garden of Eden

D. A natural antacid

2. CONTRARY TO POPULAR BELIEF, THE TOMATO IS A FRUIT, NOT A VEGETABLE. WHICH OF THESE OTHER PLANTS IS *NOT* A VEGETABLE?

A. Cucumber

B. Broccoli

C. Asparagus

D. Turnip

1.

B. To prove that tomatoes were perfectly safe, in 1820, Robert Gibbon stood on the courthouse steps in Salem, New Jersey, and ate an entire basket of tomatoes in front of the townspeople. No word on what he did to treat the heartburn that no doubt followed this exercise.

2.

A. Cucumbers are scientifically classified as fruits. They belong to the same plant family as watermelons, pumpkins, zucchini, and squash.

3. WHICH OF THE FOLLOWING WAS *NOT* ONE OF THE GENERAL MILLS MONSTER CEREALS?

A. Fruit Brute

B. Boo Berry

C. Zombie Puffs

D. Yummy Mummy

4. WHICH OF THE FOLLOWING WAS *NOT* A LIMITED-EDITION FLAVOR OF JONES SODA?

A. Turkey & Gravy

B. Salmon Paté

C. Antacid

D. Roasted Garlic Hummus

5. ONIONS BELONG TO WHAT FLOWER FAMILY?

A. Lily

B. Rose

C. Sunflower

D. Hyacinth

3.

C. And it's too bad, because Zombie Puffs would have fit right in with Count Chocula, Franken Berry, and the rest of the gang.

4.

D. We'd rather drink that than the Seahawks Collector Pack flavors Perspiration, Natural Field Turf, and Dirt...but just barely.

5.

A. Also in this very pungent family: garlic, leeks, and chives.

6. TRUE OR FALSE?

The adhesive on a lickable U.S. postage stamp contains ten calories.

7. IF YOU WENT TO A DINER AND ORDERED A "BURN THE BRITISH," WHAT WOULD YOU GET?

A. Hard-boiled eggs

B. Toasted English muffins

C. French toast

D. Short stack of pancakes

8. ALTHOUGH MILK IS THE STATE'S OFFICIAL DRINK, SOMETIMES NEBRASKANS HAVE A TASTE FOR SOMETHING A LITTLE LESS NATURAL, SO THEY INDULGE IN THE STATE'S OFFICIAL STATE SOFT DRINK. WHAT IS IT?

A. Kool-Aid

B. Pepsi

C. Country Time Lemonade

D. Dr. Pepper

6.

False. That little baby is a dietary bargain at only one-tenth of a calorie.

7.

B. And if you're in the mood for butter, you could order it "with cow to cover."

8.

A. No word on whether Kool-Aid Man had to bust through the walls at the state capital to make it happen, but Kool-Aid was designated the official soft drink in 1998.

9. **WHICH CREEPY ACTOR ALSO PENNED A GOURMET COOKBOOK?**

A. John Malkovich

B. Bela Lugosi

C. Willem Dafoe

D. Vincent Price

10. **WHICH OF THESE IS *NOT* AN ACTUAL WEEK DEDICATED TO AN OFFBEAT FOOD?**

A. Solo Diners Eat Out Week

B. Eat Dessert First Week

C. Stuff Yourself Silly Week

D. Gluten-Free Baking Week

11. **WHICH OF THESE IS *NOT* AN ACTUAL FLAVOR OF A CLASSIC SODA FOUNTAIN DRINK?**

A. Burn One in the Hay

B. Shake One in the Hay

C. Burn One All the Way

D. Shake One All the Way

79

9.

D. Long before he did the voiceover for Michael Jackson's *Thriller*, Price and his wife, Mary, penned the terrifyingly good *A Treasury of Great Recipes* (1965).

10.

C. To be fair, though, there is an Eat What You Want Day (May 11). Everything in moderation, just like we always say.

11.

A. Burn One All the Way is a chocolate malted; Shake One in the Hay is a strawberry milkshake; and Shake One All the Way is a chocolate milkshake.

12. **IS IT EVER HOT ENOUGH TO ACTUALLY FRY AN EGG ON THE SIDEWALK?**

13. **TWIST-TIES (AND PLASTIC TABS) ON BREAD SOLD IN STORES ARE COLOR-CODED. WHY?**

A. To tell which worker packaged the bread

B. To tell the date the bread was baked

C. To confuse consumers

D. To identify the bakery where the bread was baked

14. **TRUE OR FALSE?**

The Vaportini is a cocktail that you inhale instead of drink.

15. **WHAT DO THESE FOOD PHRASES ALL HAVE IN COMMON?**

A. Go hang a salami. I'm a lasagna hog.

B. A nut for a jar of tuna.

C. Ana, nab a banana.

D. Murder for a jar of red rum.

12.

No. At its hottest, even blacktop falls about 13 degrees Fahrenheit short of the 158 degrees Fahrenheit needed to host your own outdoor fry-up.

13.

B. Much to the gratitude of stock clerks everywhere, it's much easier to pick out all the twist ties of a certain color than to squint at the tiny sell-by dates on the packages when it comes time to take old bread off the shelf.

14.

True. The alcoholic experience was invented at Red Kiva, a Chicago cocktail lounge. A candle is used to heat up liquid spirits, the vapors from which are then captured in a glass ball at the top of the glass and inhaled through a straw.

15.

They're all palindromes—words or phrases that read the same forward and backward.

16. YOU'RE MILKING A COW. HOW MANY SQUIRTS OF MILK FROM THE UDDERS DOES IT TAKE TO MAKE A GALLON?

17. IN 2013, TEXAS JOINED A SHORT LIST OF STATES BY NAMING THE PECAN PIE THE OFFICIAL STATE PIE. MATCH THESE OTHER STATES WITH THEIR OFFICIAL STATE PIES.

1. Florida   **A.** Sugar cream

2. Vermont   **B.** Boston cream

3. Massachusetts   **C.** Key lime

4. Indiana   **D.** Peach

5. Delaware   **E.** Apple

18. REFRESHING LEMON-LIME SODA 7-UP ORIGINALLY COUNTED WHICH SUBSTANCE AMONG ITS INGREDIENTS?

A. Cocaine

B. Lithium

C. Valium

D. Heroin

16.

Between 340 and 350. Now imagine doing that for 10 or 15 cows twice a day for years, and you might have the makings of a farmer.

17.

1. C; 2. E; 3. B; 4. A; 5. D.

18.

B. "It's an UP thing," indeed.

19. TRUE OR FALSE?

No matter how big the ear, there are always an odd number of rows of kernels on each ear of corn.

20. AT A PRICE OF MORE THAN $300 PER POUND, KOPI LUWAK IS THE WORLD'S MOST EXPENSIVE COFFEE. WHAT MAKES THESE COFFEE BEANS SO SPECIAL?

A. Each bean is hand-roasted over an open flame.

B. Beans are only picked on the night of a blue moon.

C. Beans are picked out of animal droppings.

D. There are only five acres of fields in the world suited to grow these beans.

19.

False. Because the female flowers of corn kernels oc-
cur in pairs, there is always an even number of rows
of kernels. The better to sink your teeth into!

20.

C. Civet cats eat the coffee cherries but can't digest
the beans, so they pass through the animal's digestive tract and then are, um, handpicked and readied
for roasting.

1. IF YOU DREW A LINE WITH A STANDARD PENCIL, HOW LONG WOULD THE LINE BE BY THE TIME THE PENCIL RAN OUT OF LEAD?

A. 5 miles

B. 15 miles

C. 35 miles

D. 55 miles

2. APPROXIMATELY 20 PERCENT OF AMERICANS HAVE AN INTENSE, IRRATIONAL FEAR OF COMMON THINGS OR EXPERIENCES. WHAT IS THE NAME FOR THE FEAR OF THUNDER AND LIGHTNING?

A. Cacophobia

B. Astraphobia

C. Friggatriskaidekaphobia

D. Trypanophobia

1.

C. Or you could write about 45,000 words.

2.

B. The others are fear of ugliness (cacophobia), Friday the 13th (friggatriskaidekaphobia), and hypodermic needles (trypanophobia).

3. HOW LONG WOULD IT TAKE TO READ EVERYTHING ON THE INTERNET?

4. WHAT IS THE NAME FOR THE SPOTS ON DICE?

A. Pits

B. Pats

C. Pips

D. Spits

5. WHAT DOES A DYNAMOMETER MEASURE?

6. THE DOOMSDAY CLOCK IS A SYMBOLIC REPRESENTATION OF HOW CLOSE THE WORLD IS TO GLOBAL DISASTER (REPRESENTED BY MIDNIGHT). IT WAS LAST ADJUSTED BY *THE BULLETIN OF THE ATOMIC SCIENTISTS* IN JANUARY 2012. HOW MANY "MINUTES" ARE LEFT BEFORE TIME RUNS OUT?

A. Three

B. Four

C. Five

D. Six

3.

About six million years, according to an estimate done by the Microsoft Bing team.

4.

C. Though a bad roll really is the pits.

5.

Mechanical force—either of an engine or of a muscle contraction.

6.

C. Before you make plans for that Apocalypse Now party, consider that when the clock debuted in 1947, it was set at 11:53 p.m., a difference of only two minutes.

7. WHAT DO METEOROLOGISTS REFER TO WHEN THEY USE THE TERM "CRAWLER"?

A. Double rainbow

B. Slow-moving front

C. Tropical depression

D. Cloud-to-cloud lightning

8. WHICH OF THESE CORPORATE CATCHPHRASES HAS ITS ORIGIN IN THE MILITARY?

A. Think outside the box

B. Push the envelope

C. Let's touch base offline

D. Keep your finger on the pulse

9. HEY, YOU SITTING ON YOUR ROLLING CHAIR IN YOUR CUBICLE. HOW FAR DOES THE AVERAGE OFFICE CHAIR MOVE IN A YEAR?

A. 2 miles

B. 8 miles

C. 10 miles

D. 15 miles

7.

D. One of the longest ever recorded stretched 75 miles! Makes a plain old rainbow look downright boring, doesn't it?

8.

B. World War II test pilots listed a plane's abilities—speed, maneuverability, and engine power—on its flight envelope and constantly did their best to outperform its "limits." (We're guessing they did that at least in part by thinking outside the box.)

9.

B. Hard to believe you can come close to completing a 15k just by sitting on your duff.

10. WHAT ARE YOU DOING IF YOU LACRIMATE?

A. Belching

B. Sneezing

C. Hiccuping

D. Crying

11. WHAT DOES THE TORINO SCALE MEASURE?

A. Weight of planets

B. Chances of comets and asteroids crashing to Earth

C. Length of comets

D. Life expectancy of stars

12. TRUE OR FALSE?

A mass rush to the john during halftime of the 1984 Super Bowl caused a water main to break in Salt Lake City.

13. TRUE OR FALSE?

The human brain has enough memory capacity to store all the information in the Library of Congress.

10.

D. The technical terms for the other activities are eructation, sternutation, and singultus, respectively.

11.

B. The Torino Impact Hazard Scale goes from zero to ten, with zero being no risk ("Carry on as normal") and ten being imminent global catastrophe ("Party like it's 1999").

12.

False. It was just a coincidence—water mains broke regularly in Salt Lake City at the time—but reporters spread the story, and now people stagger their flushes...just in case.

13.

True. The total size of the collections in the Library of Congress is about 50 terabytes, while the human brain has a capacity between 1 and 1,000 terabytes.

14. **THE LAUNCH OF SPACE SHUTTLE**
DISCOVERY **WAS ONCE DELAYED AFTER**
WOODPECKERS PECKED HOLES IN THE
SPACECRAFT'S FOAM INSULATION. HOW
DID NASA SOLVE THE PROBLEM?

A. Planted bird feeders in a line leading away from the shuttle

B. Built elaborate woodpecker traps

C. Had a soldier repeatedly fire into the air

D. Installed decoy plastic owls

15. **WHICH IS THE ONLY PLANET IN OUR SOLAR**
SYSTEM *NOT* NAMED AFTER A GOD?

16. **HOW MANY GOLF BALLS ARE ON THE**
MOON?

17. **TRUE OR FALSE?**

Cockroaches would survive a nuclear blast.

14.

D. A quick trip to Wal-Mart for owl decoys was all it took to get the U.S. space mission back in the air. If only all problems were solved so easily!

15.

Earth

16.

Two. *Apollo 14* astronaut Alan Shepard hit both in 1971. And the spectacle wouldn't have been complete without advice from the peanut gallery: Mission Control offered Shepard advice on his stance, which was somewhat hampered by his space suit.

17.

False. Although they can withstand 10 times as much radiation as humans (though not as much as moths!), cockroaches aren't immune. So they might not be around to enjoy the end of the world after all.

18. WHAT DOES IT MEAN IF A GROUNDHOG SEES ITS SHADOW ON FEBRUARY 2?

A. Immediate spring

B. Six more weeks of winter

C. End of hibernation season

D. High pollen count

19. WHAT IS THE NAME FOR LITTLE LEGO PEOPLE?

A. Figurines

B. Action figures

C. Minifigs

D. Fig Newtons

20. WHAT DOES THE "WD" STAND FOR IN THE LUBRICANT WD-40?

A. Water Displacement

B. Water Department

C. Water Dispersant

D. Water Developer

18.

B. Punxsutawney Phil and his cohorts predict six more weeks of winter when they see their shadows.

19.

C. Short for "minifigures," minifigs came on the LEGO scene in 1974. At that time, they had no arms—an oversight that has thankfully been rectified.

20.

A. And the "40" represents the number of tries it took before they finally got the formula right.

GRAB BAG

1. IN A PERIOD OF WOOD AND COAL SCARCITY IN NINETEENTH-CENTURY EGYPT, WHAT PLENTIFUL RESOURCE WAS USED TO FUEL TRAINS?

A. Papyrus

B. Steam

C. Mummies

D. Lotus flowers

2. WHAT WAS THE NAME OF OLIVE OYL'S BOYFRIEND BEFORE SHE HOOKED UP WITH POPEYE?

A. Smash Tater

B. Ham Gravy

C. Leafy Green

D. Wing Turkey

1.

C. Apparently they had "mummies to burn."

2.

B. Ham Gravy hired a pipe-smoking sailor to help him on a treasure hunt, and before he knew it, the sailor was putting the "Hug-ug-ug-ug-ug-ug" on his ladylove.

3. THE TERM "TIP" AT RESTAURANTS WAS ORIGINALLY AN ACRONYM. WHAT DID IT STAND FOR?

A. To Impact Personnel

B. To Implement Purchase

C. To Increase Performance

D. To Insure Promptness

4. MATCH THE TERM WITH THE CARD GAME IT IS USED IN.

1. Stick the dealer   **A.** Bridge

2. Yarborough   **B.** Cribbage

3. Sandbagging   **C.** Euchre

4. Muggins   **D.** Hearts

5. Shoot the moon   **E.** Spades

5. THERE ARE 12 SIGNS OF THE ZODIAC. HOW MANY CAN YOU NAME?

3.

D. The phrase was written on restaurant boxes, and diners put cash in the boxes before the meal to get better service.

4.

1. C; 2. A; 3. E; 4. B; 5. D.

5.

Aries, Taurus, Gemini, Cancer, Leo, Virgo, Libra, Scorpio, Sagittarius, Capricorn, Aquarius, and Pisces

6. **WHAT TITLE DID THE FOUNDING FATHERS ORIGINALLY ASSIGN TO THE OFFICE OF THE PRESIDENT?**

A. His Highness the President of the United States of America and Protector of the Rights of the Same

B. His Royal Sovereign the President of the United States and All Her Territories

C. High Commander of these United States and the Continental Army

D. His Supremacy the President of the United States

7. **LONG BEFORE THE UNITED STATES GOT 911, GREAT BRITAIN DEVELOPED AN EMERGENCY SERVICES NUMBER. WHAT WAS IT?**

A. 999

B. 119

C. 919

D. 199

8. **THERE ARE FOUR TEENAGE MUTANT NINJA TURTLES. HOW MANY CAN YOU NAME?**

6.

A. Deciding that was too much of a mouthful—particularly for someone with such dental challenges—George Washington opted for the much simpler "Mr. President."

7.

A. The number was introduced in 1937, and a woman reporting a burglar outside her home made the first 999 call. The intruder was arrested, and the system was so successful that other countries started adopting it.

8.

Leonardo, Raphael, Donatello, and Michelangelo got their names because their creators, Kevin Eastman and Peter Laird, had both studied art history.

9. MATCH THE INFOMERCIAL PRODUCT WITH ITS CELEBRITY SPOKESPERSON.

1. Suzanne Somers　　**A.** NutriSystem

2. Chuck Norris　　　**B.** ThighMaster

3. Brooke Shields　　**C.** Tae Bo

4. Dan Marino　　　　**D.** Total Gym

5. Billy Blanks　　　**E.** Proactiv

10. WHICH OF THESE SUPPOSED APHRODISIACS IS KNOWN FOR ITS PHALLIC SHAPE?

A. Rhinoceros horn

B. Oysters

C. Ginseng root

D. Chili pepper

11. WHAT CURIOUS SUBSTANCE DID ANCIENT ROMANS USE AS A TOOTH WHITENER?

A. Urine

B. Clay

C. Grass strips

D. Crushed ants

9.

1. B; 2. D; 3. E; 4. A; 5. C.

10.

C. But don't judge it on looks alone! Ginseng has compounds that improve blood circulation—definitely a helpful attribute in this situation.

11.

A. Unsurprisingly, this practice petered out after a wee wee bit of time.

12. WHICH PEZ DISPENSER DESIGN IS THE MOST RARE?

A. Mickey Mouse

B. Bullwinkle

C. Daniel Boone

D. Mr. Potato Head

13. IN WHICH CLASSIC GAME CAN YOU BE ORDERED TO "GO DIRECTLY TO JAIL—DO NOT PASS GO, DO NOT COLLECT $200"?

A. Risk

B. Life

C. Sorry

D. Monopoly

14. WHAT IS THE MOST WIDELY SPOKEN LANGUAGE ON EARTH?

A. Spanish

B. Mandarin Chinese

C. English

D. Russian

12.

D. The detachable face pieces were deemed a choking hazard, and Pez pulled it from shelves after only a few months, making it a rare find indeed.

13.

D. You pick your card, you take your "Chance."

14.

B. There are about 1.1 billion native speakers of Mandarin. Even if you count all speakers of English (native speakers and those who speak it as a secondary language), it's still a distant second at 480 million.

15. WHAT IS THE TOP-SELLING TIE COLOR?

A. Blue

B. Red

C. Brown

D. Black

16. WHICH IS *NOT* A TOOL USED TO KEEP TIME?

A. Merkhet

B. Lathe

C. Clepsydras

D. Atomic clock

17. WHAT RAUCOUS SPRING CELEBRATION STEMS IN PART FROM THE ANCIENT ROMAN FESTIVALS OF SATURNALIA AND LUPERCALIA?

A. April Fools' Day

B. Easter Sunday

C. Mardi Gras

D. Vernal Equinox

15.

A. No word on how many of them were purchased for Father's Day.

16.

B. A merkhet is an ancient Egyptian tool used to measure time by the stars, clepsydras are water clocks, and atomic clocks measure time based on how long it takes for an atom to go from negative to positive and vice versa.

17.

C. In the spirit of "If you can't beat 'em, join 'em," early Christian leaders incorporated pagan rites of spring and fertility into this pre-Lenten day of gluttony.

18. WHICH PLANET IS HOME TO THE BIGGEST CANYON IN THE SOLAR SYSTEM?

A. Venus

B. Earth

C. Mars

D. Jupiter

19. WHICH OF THESE ANIMAL MONIKERS IS *NOT* THE NAME OF A U.S. FRATERNAL ORGANIZATION?

A. Moose

B. Elk

C. Lion

D. Cougar

20. MATCH THE AMERICAN TERM WITH ITS BRITISH EQUIVALENT.

1. Toilet paper   **A.** Draughts

2. Checkers   **B.** Plaster

3. Truck   **C.** Whinge

4. Complain   **D.** Bog roll

5. Bandage   **E.** Lorry

18.

C. Our canyon is grand, but the Martian Mariner Valley is almost 13 times longer.

19.

D. But we think it would be a great name for an order of women.

20.

1. D; 2. A; 3. E; 4. C; 5. B.

MONEY

1. CAN U.S. CURRENCY FEATURE A PORTRAIT OF A LIVING PERSON?

2. WHICH OF THESE WAS *NOT* AN EARLY FORM OF CURRENCY?

A. Cows and other livestock

B. Salt and pepper

C. Water

D. Cowry shells

3. WHAT IS THE AVERAGE LIFE EXPECTANCY FOR A ONE-DOLLAR BILL?

A. 6 months

B. 13 months

C. 21 months

D. 29 months

1.

No. An 1866 law prohibits the practice—hence the nickname "dead presidents" for money.

2.

C. Animals have long been used in trade, Roman workers were paid with salt (hence the expression "worth one's salt"), and in England in the Middle Ages, rent could be paid in peppercorns.

3.

C. Each year, 95 percent of new bills are printed to replace worn-out money.

4. WHICH BILL WEIGHS THE MOST: $1, $5, $10, $20, $50, OR $100?

---

5. WHAT IS THE LARGEST U.S. NOTE EVER PRINTED BY THE BUREAU OF ENGRAVING AND PRINTING?

A. $500 bill

B. $1,000 bill

C. $10,000 bill

D. $100,000 bill

6. HOW MANY STATES ACCEPT PENNIES AT THEIR TOLLBOOTHS?

---

7. SINCE 1787, MORE THAN 300 BILLION PENNIES HAVE BEEN PRODUCED. ABOUT HOW MANY ARE CURRENTLY IN CIRCULATION?

A. 50 billion

B. 100 billion

C. 150 billion

D. 200 billion

4.

Each bill weighs the same: one gram.

5.

D. These notes were printed in 1934 and 1935 and featured a portrait of Woodrow Wilson.

6.

One. The other 49 may not have much use for the penny, but Lincoln's home state of Illinois has a soft spot for it.

7.

C. That's enough pennies to circle Earth 137 times.

8. THE PRESIDENTIAL PROFILES ON THE PENNY, THE ORIGINAL JEFFERSON NICKEL, THE DIME, AND THE QUARTER ALL FACE LEFT EXCEPT FOR WHICH ONE?

A. Lincoln (penny)

B. Jefferson (nickel)

C. Franklin Roosevelt (dime)

D. Washington (quarter)

9. MATCH THE COUNTRY WITH ITS CURRENCY.

1. Brazil	**A.** Bolívar
2. Denmark	**B.** Real
3. Japan	**C.** Krone
4. Venezuela	**D.** Won
5. South Korea	**E.** Yen

10. WHOSE PORTRAIT WAS ON THE FIRST ONE-DOLLAR BILL MINTED BY THE U.S. TREASURY?

8.

A. People have long imagined any number of explanations for this about-face, but the disappointingly simple answer is that the sculptor was working from a photo in which Lincoln faced to the right.

9.

1. B; 2. C; 3. E; 4. A; 5. D.

10.

The honor went Treasury Secretary Salmon P. Chase when the first bill was issued in 1862. The more recognizable George Washington dollar began to be printed in 1869.

11. WHAT TIME IS SHOWN ON THE
INDEPENDENCE HALL CLOCK ON THE BACK
OF THE $100 BILL?

12. WHAT DO THE FRANC, DEUTSCHE MARK,
DRACHMA, LIRA, GUILDER, ESCUDO, AND
PESETA HAVE IN COMMON?

13. WHICH OF THESE COUNTRIES DOES *NOT*
USE THE U.S. DOLLAR AS ITS CURRENCY?

A. Zimbabwe

B. Panama

C. El Salvador

D. Zambia

14. THE CHINESE YUAN AND THE JAPANESE
YEN SHARE THE SAME ROOT WORD. WHAT
DOES IT MEAN?

A. Paper

B. Round

C. Metal

D. Golden

11.

4:10—for now, anyway. The U.S. Treasury is set to release a new, high-tech $100 bill in late 2013.

12.

All were replaced as national currency by the Euro.

13.

D. Zambia uses the kwacha.

14.

B. The word was used to describe the shape of the coinage.

15. WITH AN ESTIMATED NET WORTH OF $73 BILLION, CARLOS SLIM HELÚ OF MEXICO IS THE WORLD'S RICHEST PERSON. IN WHAT INDUSTRY DID HE MAKE HIS WEALTH?

A. Computers

B. Finance

C. Oil

D. Telecommunications

16. BILLIONAIRE WARREN BUFFETT IS THE SECOND-RICHEST VERIFIED TWITTER USER. WHO IS THE FIRST?

17. WHICH OF THE FOLLOWING IS AN EXAMPLE OF BULLION?

A. Silver bar

B. Beef futures

C. Bonds

D. Exchange traded fund

18. WHICH BILL IS REFERRED TO AS A "C-NOTE"?

15.

D. Slim gives new meaning to putting his money where his mouth is—he owns the telephone company Telmex, which operates the majority of Mexican landlines, as well as America Movil, the largest mobile carrier in Latin America.

16.

The Oracle of Omaha is second only to Microsoft founder Bill Gates.

17.

A. Although it shares the same root word with tasty broths (bouillon, meaning "boiling"), bullion refers to precious metals in bar or ingot form.

18.

The $100 bill—C is the Roman numeral for 100. The bill is also sometimes called a "Benjamin," in reference to the image of Benjamin Franklin on the front.

19. You have one hundred $20 bills in your hand. How many of them are likely to be counterfeit?

20. True or false?

Trace amounts of cocaine can be found on about 90 percent of paper money in U.S. cities.

19.

Two. According to the U.S. Secret Service, a little less than 2 percent of American money is counterfeit, and $20 bills are popular targets, particularly for domestic counterfeiters. International counterfeiters tend to be more high rollers and prefer to mint their own $100 bills.

20.

True. But that's not even the worst thing that's on your dirty money! About 94 percent of bills carry pathogens like staphylococcus, making your money more germ-filled than the average toilet.

1. **CLINT EASTWOOD WAS FAR FROM THE STUDIO'S FIRST CHOICE TO "MAKE THEIR DAY" AS *DIRTY HARRY*. WHICH OF THESE ACTORS WAS *NOT* OFFERED THE ROLE BEFORE EASTWOOD?**

A. Frank Sinatra

B. John Wayne

C. Robert Redford

D. Paul Newman

2. **WHICH OF THESE HISTORICAL FIGURES HAS BEEN FEATURED IN THE MOST MOVIES?**

A. Jesus Christ

B. Abraham Lincoln

C. King Henry VIII

D. Napoleon Bonaparte

125

MOVIES

QUESTIONS

1.

C. When Eastwood was finally offered the role, he felt very lucky indeed.

2.

D. The "little general" has more than 194 movies to his credit.

3. MATCH THE ACTOR WITH HIS OR HER STAGE NAME.

1. Yul Brynner   **A.** Issur Demsky

2. Divine   **B.** Taidje Khan

3. Whoopi Goldberg   **C.** Joyce Frankenberg

4. Kirk Douglas   **D.** Caryn Johnson

5. Jane Seymour   **E.** Glenn Milstead

4. WHICH OF THESE STARS IS *NOT* A TWIN?

A. Scarlett Johansson (*Hitchcock*)

B. Vin Diesel (*Fast & Furious*)

C. Jon Heder (*Napoleon Dynamite*)

D. Ryan Gosling (*Gangster Squad*)

5. SIX ACTORS HAVE PLAYED JAMES BOND IN THE EON PRODUCTIONS OFFICIAL MOVIE SERIES. HOW MANY OF THEM CAN YOU NAME?

3.

1. B; 2. E; 3. D; 4. A; 5. C.

4.

D. Hey girl (or guy!), Ryan Gosling's no twin.

5.

They are: Sean Connery, George Lazenby, Roger Moore, Timothy Dalton, Pierce Brosnan, and Daniel Craig.

6. HOW MANY ACTORS DID IT TAKE TO PORTRAY DARTH VADER IN *STAR WARS*?

7. OSCAR WINNER HILLARY SWANK MADE HER FILM DEBUT IN THE CAMPY 1992 FILM VERSION OF *BUFFY THE VAMPIRE SLAYER*. WHICH OTHER FUTURE OSCAR WINNER WAS PART OF THE MOVIE'S CAST?

A. Heath Ledger

B. Jamie Foxx

C. Ben Affleck

D. Adrien Brody

8. WHICH CLASSIC VIDEO GAME CHARACTER DID *NOT* MAKE A CAMEO APPEARANCE IN DISNEY'S *WRECK-IT RALPH*?

A. Q*bert

B. Sonic the Hedgehog

C. Mario

D. Pac-Man

6.

Four. James Earl Jones provided Vader's deep, booming voice; David Prowse played the villain's body; Sebastian Shaw played the unmasked face; and sound designer Ben Burtt provided the dark lord's infamous breathing effect.

7.

C. Affleck had an uncredited role and only one line as "Basketball Player #10"—and five years later co-wrote the screenplay for *Good Will Hunting*, for which he earned his first Oscar. You've come a long way, Ben!

8.

C. His nemesis Bowser makes an appearance at a meeting of BAD-ANON (a support group for video game villains), but everyone's favorite plumber will just have to wait for the sequel to make his appearance.

9. **IN WHICH OF THESE MOVIES IS THE F-BOMB DROPPED THE MOST?**

A. *Casino*

B. *Scarface*

C. *Alpha Dog*

D. *Summer of Sam*

10. **WHICH SCARY MOVIE WAS *NOT* BASED ON A BOOK PENNED BY STEPHEN KING?**

A. *Carrie*

B. *Poltergeist*

C. *Children of the Corn*

D. *The Green Mile*

11. **TO WHAT SONG DOES PHIL CONNORS WAKE EVERY MORNING IN *GROUNDHOG DAY*?**

A. "I Got You Babe" by Sonny and Cher

B. "Homeward Bound" by Simon and Garfunkel

C. "These Boots Are Made for Walkin'" by Nancy Sinatra

D. "California Dreamin'" by The Mamas & The Papas

9.

D. When it was released in 1983, *Scarface* had a record 226 instances of the word, but Spike Lee's 1999 movie *Summer of Sam* used the F-word a whopping 435 times, or 3.06 times per minute.

10.

B. This ghost story was coauthored by another writing heavyweight named Steven—Spielberg, that is.

11.

A. By some estimates, Bill Murray's character wakes up to the song for a full 34 years during the film. How's that for an earworm?

12. TRUE OR FALSE?

In the original script for *E.T. the Extra-Terrestrial*, the adorable alien dies.

13. ARNOLD SWARZENEGGER IS ONE OF ONLY TWO CALIFORNIA GOVERNORS TO HAVE BEEN AWARDED A STAR ON THE HOLLYWOOD WALK OF FAME. WHO IS THE OTHER?

14. WHICH ACTOR HAS WON THE MOST ACADEMY AWARDS IN THE CATEGORY ACTOR IN A LEADING ROLE?

A. Tom Hanks

B. Jack Nicholson

C. Daniel Day-Lewis

D. Gene Hackman

15. IN HOW MANY MOVIES DID JOHN WAYNE DIE?

12.

True. Children hated the original ending, so director Steven Spielberg changed the script so the lovable E.T. could go back home.

13.

Ronald Reagan, who is also the only U.S. president to have received the honor.

14.

C. Day-Lewis has three; the others have two wins in the category. Not bad for a man who has had only five film roles in the past 10 years!

15.

Seven: *Reap the Wild Wind, The Fighting Seabees, Wake of the Red Witch, Sands of Iwo Jima, The Alamo, The Cowboys,* and *The Shootist*

16. WHICH OF THESE FILMS IS *NOT* PART OF THE *LORD OF THE RINGS* TRILOGY?

A. *The Hobbit*

B. *The Return of the King*

C. *The Fellowship of the Ring*

D. *The Two Towers*

17. WHAT IS THE REAL FIRST NAME OF INDIANA JONES?

A. Max

B. Henry

C. Frank

D. Joe

18. HEDWIG, HARRY POTTER'S PET IN THE BOOKS AND MOVIE SERIES, IS WHAT KIND OF ANIMAL?

A. Owl

B. Ferret

C. Cat

D. Guinea pig

16.

A. *The Hobbit: An Unexpected Journey* (2012) is the first in a new trilogy. Director Peter Jackson brings to life another classic book by J.R.R. Tolkien.

17.

B. The nickname came from Jones's childhood dog (who was in turn named for a dog owned by series creator George Lucas).

18.

A. Hedwig was given to Harry as a birthday gift, and becomes his companion and messenger.

19. IN THE CLASSIC MEL BROOKS FILM *BLAZING SADDLES* (1974), WHAT LAST NAME IS SHARED BY ALL THE CITIZENS OF ROCK RIDGE?

A. Smith

B. Jones

C. Johnson

D. Doe

20. MATCH THE ACTOR TO THE MOVIE IN WHICH HE PLAYED SANTA.

1. Tim Allen   **A.** *Elf*

2. Billy Bob Thornton   **B.** *Bad Santa*

3. Edmund Gwenn   **C.** *Fred Claus*

4. Ed Asner   **D.** *The Santa Clause*

5. Paul Giamatti   **E.** *Miracle on 34th Street*

19.

C. The last name emphasizes the homogeneity of the all-white town before black sheriff Bart is brought in by scheming politicos intent on destroying the town.

20.

1. D; 2. B; 3. E; 4. A; 5. C.

MUSIC

1. WHICH FAIRY TALE INSPIRED DURAN DURAN'S HIT SONG "HUNGRY LIKE THE WOLF"?

A. *The Wolf and the Seven Little Kids*

B. *The Three Little Pigs*

C. *The Wolf and the Man*

D. *Little Red Riding Hood*

2. IN THE SIMON AND GARFUNKEL SONG OF THE SAME NAME, WHY DOES THE NARRATOR NEED TO GO "SOMEWHERE THEY CAN'T FIND ME"?

A. He had a fight with his brother.

B. He robbed a liquor store.

C. He escaped from prison.

D. His lover broke his heart.

1.

D. "Hungry Like the Wolf" was the second single from the 1982 album *Rio*.

2.

B. The narrator leaves his lover in the middle of the night to avoid being arrested.

3. **METALLICA'S 1990S SMASH HIT "ENTER SANDMAN" FEATURES THE REPEATING LYRIC "WE'RE OFF TO NEVER-NEVER LAND." WHAT LYRIC DID SINGER JAMES HETFIELD ORIGINALLY WRITE INSTEAD OF THIS CATCHPHRASE?**

A. "Maybe it's not meant to be."

B. "Disrupt the perfect family."

C. "Dream in perfect ecstasy."

D. "Nightmares help you really see."

4. **U2'S HIT SONG "PRIDE (IN THE NAME OF LOVE)" FEATURES THESE LYRICS IN REFERENCE TO THE ASSASSINATION OF DR. MARTIN LUTHER KING, JR.: "EARLY MORNING, APRIL FOUR/SHOT RINGS OUT IN THE MEMPHIS SKY..." WHY SHOULDN'T LISTENERS RELY ON BONO FOR THEIR HISTORY LESSONS?**

A. King wasn't killed in Memphis.

B. King died in May.

C. The assassination took place in the evening.

D. King wasn't shot.

3.

B. The band decided the lyric was too dark for the song to succeed and convinced Hetfield to change it—and the rest, as they say, is RIAA Certified Platinum single history.

4.

C. Bono now sings, "Early evening, April four" in live shows.

5. MATCH THE RAPPER WITH HIS OR HER STAGE NAME.

1. Shawntae Harris

2. Curtis Jackson

3. Dana Owens

4. Calvin Broadus

5. Shawn Carter

A. 50 Cent

B. Snoop Dogg

C. Jay Z

D. Da Brat

E. Queen Latifah

6. WHAT PATRIOTICALLY TITLED ALBUM WAS THE FIRST COMPACT DISC EVER MADE IN THE UNITED STATES?

A. *Breakfast in America*, Supertramp

B. *America (The Way I See It)*, Hank Williams, Jr.

C. *Born in the U.S.A.*, Bruce Springsteen

D. *Back in the USA*, MC5

5.

1. D; 2. A; 3. E; 4. B; 5. C.

6.

C. The Boss's 1984 release shares the record for most top ten hits (seven) from a single album with *Thriller* (Michael Jackson, 1982) and *Rhythm Nation 1814* (Janet Jackson, 1989).

7. WHO WAS THE INSPIRATION FOR THE DUDE IN AEROSMITH'S "DUDE (LOOKS LIKE A LADY)"?

A. Vince Neil (Mötley Crüe)

B. Jon Bon Jovi (Bon Jovi)

C. Dee Snider (Twisted Sister)

D. Sebastian Bach (Skid Row)

8. WHO IS THE ONLY MALE COUNTRY MUSIC STAR TO HAVE EXCEEDED TEN MILLION SALES FOR FOUR DIFFERENT ALBUMS?

A. Johnny Cash

B. Garth Brooks

C. Willie Nelson

D. Kenny Chesney

9. WHICH BAND DID *NOT* FEATURE LEGENDARY GUITARIST ERIC CLAPTON?

A. The Yardbirds

B. Traffic

C. Cream

D. Derek and the Dominos

7.

A. The song was released in 1987 at the height of the "hair bands." Go ahead, Google it. We'll wait.

8.

B. Perhaps his "Friends in Low Places" were hanging out at the record shop.

9.

B. Steve Winwood, who formed Traffic with three friends, later went on to form the band Blind Faith with Clapton.

10. WHICH OF THESE MUSICAL ACTS TURNED DOWN THE CHANCE TO PERFORM AT THE 1969 WOODSTOCK MUSIC AND ART FESTIVAL?

A. The Grateful Dead

B. Sly & the Family Stone

C. Jethro Tull

D. Jefferson Airplane

11. WHICH OF THESE MUSICIANS IS *NOT* A NATIVE CANADIAN?

A. Alanis Morissette

B. Neil Young

C. Celine Dion

D. Van Morrison

12. WHAT AMERICAN CITY IS MOST ASSOCIATED WITH GRUNGE MUSIC?

A. New York

B. Memphis

C. Seattle

D. Minneapolis

147

10.

C. In an interview, front man Ian Anderson cited his aversion to hippies and spontaneous outdoor nudity as reasons for turning down the gig.

11.

D. The "Brown Eyed Girl" singer was born in Belfast, Ireland.

12.

C. Seattle produced grunge rockers Pearl Jam, Alice in Chains, Soundgarden, and of course, Nirvana.

13. **OZZY OSBOURNE WAS FAMOUSLY BANNED FROM THE CITY OF SAN ANTONIO FOR A DECADE. WHAT DID HE DO TO EARN HIS BANISHMENT?**

A. Bit the head off a live bat in a concert there

B. Gave a lewd, nude public performance

C. Urinated on the Alamo

D. Started a riot

14. **WHICH PIANO-PLAYING ENTERTAINER EARNED THE NICKNAMES "MR. SHOWMANSHIP" AND "THE GLITTER MAN"?**

A. Stevie Wonder

B. Liberace

C. Elton John

D. Billy Joel

15. **WHICH MUSICAL GENRE HAS THE MOST RADIO STATIONS IN THE UNITED STATES?**

A. Rock

B. Top 40

C. Country

D. Oldies

13.

C. Osbourne acted in a drunken stupor, but later made up with the city by donating $20,000 to the Daughters of the Republic of Texas to help restore the national landmark. We bet Ozzy doesn't have any trouble remembering the Alamo these days!

14.

B. Liberace's legendary bedazzled pianos were no match for his wardrobe, which included such gems as a blue fox cape that trailed 16 feet behind him and a King Neptune costume that weighed 200 pounds.

15.

C. There are nearly 2,000 country stations around the country. That's a lot of twang!

16. **MUSIC LEGEND BOB DYLAN HAD WHAT BODY PART INSURED BY LLOYD'S OF LONDON?**

A. Vocal cords

B. Throat

C. Hands

D. Fingers

17. **WHICH HEIGHT-CHALLENGED SINGER WAS PARODIED IN AN INFAMOUS BASKETBALL SKIT ON *CHAPPELLE'S SHOW*?**

A. David Bowie

B. Cee Lo Green

C. Lil Wayne

D. Prince

18. **WHICH FORMER BEATLE WAS THE FIRST PERSON TO BE FEATURED ON THE COVER OF *ROLLING STONE*?**

A. George Harrison

B. Paul McCartney

C. John Lennon

D. Ringo Starr

16.

A. Dylan was apparently worried that the day would come when he would stop blowin' in the wind.

17.

D. In the skit, Charlie Murphy tells a story about being beaten in basketball by Prince and his crew, who were still wearing their stage costumes (picture a purple velvet suit and heeled boots). After the skit aired, Prince said in interviews that while he wasn't really wearing a costume, he really did school Murphy on the court.

18

C. No, it wasn't the naked picture with Yoko Ono—in 1967, Lennon was featured in a still from the film *How I Won the War*.

PLANES, TRAINS & AUTOMOBILES

1. WHICH OF THE FOLLOWING WAS NOT A
TRANSPORTATION OPTION FOR BARBIE?

A. Dazzling pink Jaguar XJS convertible

B. Barbie Party Cruise ship

C. United Airlines Barbie Friend Ship plane

D. Barbie Glamorous Greyhound bus

2. WHAT IS THE NICKNAME GIVEN TO THE
AIRPLANE USED BY NASA TO TRAIN
ASTRONAUTS IN A ZERO-GRAVITY
ENVIRONMENT?

A. Tummy Twister

B. Invertigo

C. Vomit Comet

D. Iron Constitution

1.

D. Even Barbie couldn't make the bus fun!

2.

C. But those who have a greater sense of propriety call it the Weightless Wonder.

3. WHICH PRESIDENT WAS THE FIRST TO TRAVEL EXTENSIVELY BY PLANE?

A. Herbert Hoover

B. Franklin Roosevelt

C. Harry Truman

D. Dwight Eisenhower

4. THE JAPANESE OHKA ("CHERRY BLOSSOM") AIRPLANE WAS DESIGNED SPECIFICALLY FOR SUICIDE ATTACKS IN WORLD WAR II. WHAT UNIQUE FEATURE DID IT HAVE?

A. It could only fly a preprogrammed route.

B. It couldn't take off or land.

C. It had an extra set of wings.

D. It had no front window for the pilot to see from.

5. ON WHICH DAY OF THE WEEK DO THE MOST CAR ACCIDENTS TAKE PLACE?

6. TRUE OR FALSE?

The *Peanuts* comic strip was first animated for a Ford commercial.

3.

B. Roosevelt did a lot of air travel to Europe, particularly in support of the World War II effort.

4.

B. The Cherry Blossom had to be carried into battle by a medium bomber. Fortunately, U.S. warplanes were quick on the draw and tended to shoot down the bombers, so the Ohka did relatively little harm.

5.

Forget about Sunday drivers—it's the ones driving on Saturdays you have to watch out for.

6.

True. In the 1959 commercial, Charlie Brown passes out (chocolate) cigars to all his friends to celebrate a new Ford economy model.

7. WHICH VEHICLE IS THE MOST STOLEN MODEL?

A. Nissan Sentra

B. Chevrolet Silverado

C. Honda Accord

D. Ford Explorer

8. WHICH OF THESE IS *NOT* A HYBRID AUTO?

A. Chevrolet Volt

B. Nissan Leaf

C. Toyota Prius

D. Honda Insight

9. WHAT IS THE LAND SPEED RECORD FOR MOTORCYCLES?

A. 350.8 miles per hour

B. 358.9 miles per hour

C. 363.2 miles per hour

D. 376.3 miles per hour

7.

C. The car is particularly popular with thieves who don't want to call attention to their activities.

8.

B. The Nissan Leaf, launched in December 2010, is a completely electric car: no gas, no tailpipe, and no emissions.

9.

D. In 2006, the record was 350.8 miles per hour, but Rocky Robinson brought it up to 376.3 miles per hour in September 2010 riding the Ack Attack, a specially designed streamliner.

10. WHICH COUNTRY HAS THE FASTEST TRAINS ON WHEELS?

A. United States

B. France

C. Japan

D. Netherlands

11. WHICH TYPE OF CLASSIC TRAIN CAR HAS BEEN ALL BUT PHASED OUT?

A. Dining car

B. Sleeping car

C. Baggage car

D. Caboose

12. WHAT IS THE NICKNAME FOR THE UNDERSEA RAIL TUNNEL THAT CONNECTS LONDON AND PARIS?

A. Chunnel

B. Charger

C. Channel

D. Changer

10.

B. The French TGV can travel as fast as 357.2 miles per hour.

11.

D. The caboose has just about reached the end of the line as a result of technological advances that mean gadgets can check the tracks for trouble and operate switches and brakes instead of people.

12.

A. The Chunnel consists of 23 miles of tubes that take passengers under the English Channel in a mere 20 minutes (a ferry crossing takes about 75 minutes). All told, it takes only 2 hours and 15 minutes on board the Chunnel Train to get from Paris to London or vice versa.

13. WHICH COUNTRY PRODUCES THE MOST PASSENGER CARS IN THE WORLD?

A. Germany

B. United States

C. China

D. Japan

14. MATCH THE CB RADIO SLANG EXPRESSION USED BY TRUCKERS WITH ITS MEANING.

1. Salt shaker

2. Bear bait

3. Draggin' wagon

4. Evel Knievel

5. Chicken coop

A. Motorcycle officer

B. Snow plow

C. Weigh station

D. Speeding car

E. Tow truck

13.

C. China produces a whopping one out of every four new passenger cars in the world.

14

1. B; 2. D; 3. E; 4. A; 5. C.

15. ONE OF THE MOST FAMOUS CINEMATIC CAR CHASES TOOK PLACE IN THE 1968 MOVIE *BULLITT.* CAN YOU NAME THE MAKES AND MODELS OF THE TWO CARS?

16. IN 2012, DRIVER DAN RUNTE SET A NEW WORLD RECORD BY JUMPING 214 FEET, 8 INCHES—THE LONGEST JUMP MADE BY A MONSTER TRUCK. WHAT DID THE TRUCK JUMP OVER?

A. Airplane

B. Ten other monster trucks

C. Six buses

D. Nothing

17. THE NAMESAKE SON OF WHICH POLITICIAN CO-PILOTED THE FIRST CIRCUMNAVIGATION OF THE GLOBE BY HELICOPTER?

A. George H. W. Bush

B. Ross Perot

C. Dan Quayle

D. Joe Biden

15.

Ford Mustang and Dodge Charger

16.

D. Since the jump was being recorded for posterity, it took place on a dirt track marked with white lines.

17.

B. With more than a little help from his famous father—including arranging for a refueling station in the middle of the Pacific—Ross Perot Jr. made the 30-day trip in 1982.

18. WHICH STATE HAS THE MOST SHIPWRECKS PER SQUARE MILE?

A. Rhode Island

B. Michigan

C. California

D. Florida

19. WHAT IS THE WORLD'S CHEAPEST NEW CAR AS OF 2013?

A. Yugo

B. Smart

C. Tata Nano

D. Mini Cooper

20. WHAT IS THE MOST EXPENSIVE STREET CAR EVER MADE?

A. Aston Martin One-77

B. Koenigsegg CCXR

C. Ferrari Enzo

D. Lamborghini Reventon

18.

A. At least 2,000 shipwrecks have been discovered in the tiny state...so far.

19.

C. The tiny $2,600 price tag matches the super compact body of the Nano.

20.

B. This Swedish car is hand-built and goes from zero to sixty in 2.9 seconds—a bargain, really, at $2,173,950.

TELEVISION

1. WHICH HIT SONG WAS BANNED FROM *AMERICAN IDOL* AUDITIONS AFTER JUDGES GOT TIRED OF HEARING IT GET BUTCHERED?

A. "Rolling in the Deep," Adele

B. "Proud Mary," Tina Turner

C. "Fallin,'" Alicia Keys

D. "I Will Always Love You," Whitney Houston

2. IN WHICH PBS CHILDREN'S SHOW DID A TROLLEY TRANSPORT VIEWERS TO THE NEIGHBORHOOD OF MAKE BELIEVE?

A. *Sesame Street*

B. *The Electric Company*

C. *Mister Rogers' Neighborhood*

D. *Reading Rainbow*

167

1.

C. Too many contestants couldn't hit the right *Keys*.

2.

C. The puppets in the Neighborhood of Make Believe were named for important people in Rogers's life, including Queen Sara Saturday (his wife), Harriet Elizabeth Cow (his aunt), and Lady Elaine Fairchilde (his sister).

3. WILLIAM HUNG GOT HIS 15 MINUTES OF FAME BY BEING A SPECTACULARLY BAD *AMERICAN IDOL* HOPEFUL. WHAT SONG DID HE SING FOR HIS AUDITION?

4. WHICH *DOCTOR WHO* ALSO HAD A ROLE IN *HARRY POTTER AND THE GOBLET OF FIRE*?

A. Paul McGann

B. Christopher Eccleston

C. David Tennant

D. Matt Smith

5. HE'S NOT A DOCTOR, BUT HE PLAYS THEM (OR TRIES TO) ON TV. WHICH ROLE DID PATRICK DEMPSEY AUDITION FOR BEFORE LANDING THE ROLE OF MCDREAMY HIMSELF, DR. DEREK SHEPHERD, ON *GREY'S ANATOMY*?

A. Dr. Jack Hodgins, *Bones*

B. Dr. Mark Greene, *ER*

C. Dr. Robert Chase, *House*

D. Dr. Sean McNamara, *Nip/Tuck*

3.

Hung's rendition of Ricky Martin's "She Bangs" won him a huge following, but haunts us to this day.

4.

C. Tennant played Barty Crouch Jr., a wizard who left Hogwart's to join the evil forces of Lord Voldemort in the film.

5.

C. Hmm, we're not feeling it. We could see him rocking the role of Dr. Wilson, though.

6. **WHICH OF THESE CLASSICS IS GENERALLY CONSIDERED TO BE THE FIRST REALITY TV SHOW?**

A. *Truth or Consequences*

B. *Candid Camera*

C. *I've Got a Secret*

D. *To Tell the Truth*

7. **WHAT ARE THE NAMES OF MARGE'S OLDER SISTERS ON *THE SIMPSONS*?**

A. Lori and Bertha

B. Annie and Melba

C. Patty and Selma

D. Jackie and Diana

8. **WHICH TRAILBLAZING COMEDIAN GOT HER BIG BREAK WITH THE PARODY SONG "I MADE A FOOL OF MYSELF OVER JOHN FOSTER DULLES"?**

A. Carol Burnett

B. Phyllis Diller

C. Joan Rivers

D. Betty White

171

6.

B. The *Punked* of its day, Allen Funt's hidden camera/practical joke series premiered in 1948.

7.

C. Marge's chain-smoking, Homer-hating twin sisters live together at the Spinster Arms apartment complex and work at the DMV.

8.

A. The ode to the then–U.S. Secretary of State garnered major attention for Burnett in 1957, and she was invited to perform on *The Tonight Show* and *The Ed Sullivan Show* that year.

9. WHICH TALK SHOW HOST HAS CORNERED THE MARKET ON PUBLIC PATERNITY TESTS, PROCLAIMING DRAMATICALLY "YOU ARE/ ARE NOT THE FATHER" AS THE RESULTS ARE REVEALED?

A. Ricki Lake

B. Maury Povich

C. Jerry Springer

D. Montel Williams

10. AFTER 15 SEASONS OF SASSY TV COURTROOM DRAMA, CBS CANCELED WHICH JUDGE'S SHOW IN 2013 OVER A SALARY DISPUTE?

A. Judith Sheindlin (*Judge Judy*)

B. Greg Mathis (*Judge Mathis*)

C. Jeanine Pirro (*Judge Pirro*)

D. Joseph Brown (*Judge Joe Brown*)

11. HOW MANY SISTERS DOES JOEY TRIBIANI HAVE ON *FRIENDS*?

9.

B. We have the results right here in our hands: Maury Povich, you ARE the answer.

10.

D. Judge Brown claimed he was promised a salary of $20 million per year but the network didn't pay up. Perhaps he should take them to court...*The People's Court.*

11.

Seven: Veronica, Mary Angela, Mary Theresa, Gina, Dina, Tina, and Cookie

12. WHAT WAS THE NAME OF THE IN-HOUSE BAND ON *THE MUPPET SHOW*?

A. Extraordinary Chaos

B. Electric Mayhem

C. Eclectic Bedlam

D. Endearing Pandemonium

13. WHICH GAME ON THE LONG-RUNNING SHOW *THE PRICE IS RIGHT* REQUIRES CONTESTANTS TO EARN CHIPS, THEN SLIDE THEM DOWN A PEGBOARD IN ATTEMPT TO LAND ON A BIG CASH PRIZE?

A. Showcase Showdown

B. Plinko

C. Pass the Buck

D. Hi Lo

14. WHAT FICTIONAL COMPANY COUNTS WILE E. COYOTE AMONG ITS BEST CUSTOMERS?

A. Amway

B. Acme

C. Arrow

D. Atlantis

12.

B. Led by Dr. Teeth, the band included Sgt. Floyd Pepper on the bass, Janice on lead guitar and vocals, and, of course, Animal on the drums.

13.

B. The top prize for Plinko is $2,500—unless you are a lucky contestant who "comes on down" during Big Money Week, when the top prize is doubled to $5,000.

14.

B. The shady Acme company specialized in inventions designed to help capture Road Runner.

15. **IF YOU HIRED THE FIRM STERLING COOPER DRAPER PRYCE, WHAT SERVICES WOULD YOU GET?**

A. Legal counsel

B. Crisis management

C. Advertising

D. Architecture and design

16. **ON WHICH SHORT-LIVED CARTOON DID DISGRACED 1980S POP DUO MILLI VANILLI MAKE A GUEST APPEARANCE?**

A. *The Adventures of Super Mario Bros. 3*

B. *Bill & Ted's Excellent Adventures*

C. *Pole Position*

D. *Alf's Animated Adventures*

17. **WHICH BRITISH TV SERIES HAS BEEN NOMINATED FOR THE MOST EMMY AWARDS?**

A. *Sherlock*

B. *Doctor Who*

C. *Monty Python's Flying Circus*

D. *Downton Abbey*

15.

C. The men and women of *Mad Men* know how to sell a product—especially a cable TV show!

16.

A. Rob and Fab were kidnapped by Bowser's minions and brought back to the castle for a command live performance. You can guess how *that* turned out.

17.

D. In its first two seasons alone, the period drama was nominated for a whopping 27 Emmys.

18. **WHICH CAST MEMBER OF *GIRLS* DOES *NOT* HAVE A FAMOUS PARENT?**

A. Zosia Mamet

B. Jemima Kirke

C. Allison Williams

D. Lena Dunham

19. **MATCH THE TV STAR WITH HIS OR HER PRE-CELEBRITY OCCUPATION.**

1. David Letterman

2. Whoopi Goldberg

3. Dennis Farina

4. Paula Abdul

5. Jason Lee

A. Competitive skateboarder

B. Police officer

C. LA Lakers cheerleader

D. TV news weather person

E. Bricklayer

20. **WHICH COUPLE WERE THE FIRST TO BE SHOWN IN BED TOGETHER ON PRIMETIME AMERICAN TELEVISION?**

A. Fred and Wilma Flintstone (*The Flintstones*)

B. Mike and Carol Brady (*The Brady Bunch*)

C. Lucy and Ricky Ricardo (*I Love Lucy*)

D. Samantha and Darren Stevens (*Bewitched*)

18.

D. Mamet's father is playwright David Mamet; Kirke's father is drummer Simon Kirke; and Williams's father is news anchor Brian Williams.

19.

1. D; 2. B; 3. E; 4. C; 5. A.

20.

A. Amazingly enough, the town of Bedrock (and the rest of America) didn't take to the fainting couches in shock at the sight.

WHERE IN THE WORLD

1. WHAT IS THE MOST POPULOUS CITY IN NORTH AMERICA?

A. Toronto

B. New York City

C. Mexico City

D. Los Angeles

2. IN WHICH OCEAN CAN YOU FIND A MASSIVE "ISLAND" MADE ENTIRELY OF GARBAGE?

A. Indian

B. Pacific

C. Atlantic

D. Arctic

3. TRUE OR FALSE?

The Dead Sea is the world's saltiest body of water.

1.

C. With a population of 8.85 million, Mexico City beats out all the competition.

2.

B. The Great Pacific Garbage Patch covers an area about 100 feet deep and as much as one and a half times the land area of the United States. That is a *hefty* amount of garbage.

3.

False. The Dead Sea's salinity is 340 grams per liter, but Lake Asal in the East African country of Djibouti blows that out of the water with a salinity of 400 grams per liter. But before you think about bobbing in its curative waters, keep in mind that Lake Asal has a salt crust up to 13 inches thick along its "shore"—thick enough to drive a car on!

4. **WHICH IS THE ONLY CITY IN THE WORLD TO HAVE TURNED DOWN A CHANCE TO HOST THE OLYMPICS?**

A. Denver, Colorado, USA

B. St. Petersburg, Russia

C. Istanbul, Turkey

D. Madrid, Spain

5. **THE DEEPEST AREA IN THE WORLD'S OCEANS SHARES A NAME WITH WHICH SPACE SHUTTLE?**

A. *Atlantis*

B. *Challenger*

C. *Columbia*

D. *Discovery*

6. **WHAT EUROPEAN CAPITAL IS HOME TO MORE DOGS THAN PEOPLE?**

A. London

B. Berlin

C. Paris

D. Amsterdam

183

4.

A. Residents of the Mile-High City took to the ballot and voted against holding the 1976 Winter Games in their city. Not to worry, though—the city and state have formed a committee to consider a bid for the 2022 Winter Games.

5.

B. Challenger Deep is named after the ship whose crew discovered the depth—nearly seven miles—of this part of the Pacific Ocean.

6.

C. When visiting the French capital, *attention à la marche* (watch your step).

7. WHERE IS THE WORLD'S LARGEST ICE SKATING AREA?

A. Ottawa, Ontario, Canada

B. Vaasa, Finland

C. Moscow, Russia

D. Nuuk, Greenland

8. WHAT IS THE MOST REMOTE ISLAND IN THE WORLD?

A. Saint Helena

B. Bouvet Island

C. Easter Island

D. Kiribati

9. THE G8 IS A GROUP OF EIGHT POWERFUL COUNTRIES WHOSE REPRESENTATIVES MEET EACH YEAR TO TRY TO SOLVE GLOBAL PROBLEMS. HOW MANY OF THE EIGHT COUNTRIES CAN YOU NAME?

10. WHAT IS THE ONLY ONE OF THE SEVEN WONDERS OF THE ANCIENT WORLD STILL IN EXISTENCE?

7.

A. If you've got the time and the stamina, you can skate 4.8 miles on Ottawa's Rideau Canal Skateway.

8.

B. This South Atlantic island is almost a thousand miles away from its closest neighbor, Queen Maude Land, Antarctica. If you need to borrow a cup of sugar, though, you're out of luck—the island is uninhabited.

9.

Canada, France, Germany, Italy, Japan, Russia, United Kingdom, and United States

10.

The Great Pyramid of Giza. The other six wonders—the Colossus of Rhodes, the Hanging Gardens of Babylon, the lighthouse at Alexandria, the mausoleum at Halicarnassus, the statue of Zeus at Olympia, and the Temple of Artemis at Ephesus—are lost to the sands of time.

11. WHAT IS THE COLLECTIVE NAME FOR THE VAST RURAL AREAS OF AUSTRALIA?

A. Great Plains

B. Big Steppes

C. Outback

D. Centrelands

12. WHAT IS THE CAPITAL OF TURKEY?

A. Ankara

B. Istanbul

C. Bursa

D. Adana

13. WHICH IS THE LARGEST CONTINENT?

A. North America

B. Antarctica

C. Africa

D. Asia

14. TRUE OR FALSE?

There are two European countries that are smaller than New York's Central Park.

187

11.

C. It's not just a great steakhouse! The Outback is also nicknamed "the back of beyond" and "beyond the black stump."

12.

A. This planned city beat out its big sister Istanbul because of its position right in the center of the country—much to the Turkish delight of its residents!

13.

D. Asia is the largest both by land mass (44,579,000 square miles) and population (4 billion).

14.

True. Central Park covers 1.3 square miles, while Monaco covers 0.7 square miles and the tiny nation of Vatican City only occupies 0.2 square miles.

15. **WHICH SOUTH AMERICAN COUNTRY IS HOME TO THE ANCIENT CITY OF MACHU PICCHU?**

A. Brazil

B. Colombia

C. Bolivia

D. Peru

16. **AMSTERDAM IS SOMETIMES CALLED THE "VENICE OF THE NORTH." HOW MANY CANALS DOES IT HAVE?**

A. 55

B. 105

C. 165

D. 215

17. **WHAT IS THE ONLY COUNTRY WITH A FLAG THAT IS *NOT* RECTANGULAR OR SQUARE?**

A. Yemen

B. Nepal

C. Switzerland

D. Mexico

15.

D. The ancient home of the Inca Empire used to be a six-day walk from civilization, but now train travelers can leave from Cusco and get there in mere hours.

16.

C. And along with the canals are 1,281 bridges, most of which open to let ships pass through and provide Dutch schoolchildren with a handy "The bridge was open" excuse for tardiness. Hey, it beats "The dog ate my homework."

17.

B. Nepal's flag is made of two joined triangular shapes with sun and moon designs.

18. THE UNITED STATES HAS SHORELINE ON HOW MANY OCEANS?

19. WHICH LANDMARK SHRINKS ABOUT SIX INCHES EVERY WINTER?

A. Big Ben

B. Leaning Tower of Pisa

C. Eiffel Tower

D. Giralda Tower

20. ON SEPTEMBER 3, 1967, SWEDEN SWITCHED SIDES—WHICH SIDE OF THE ROAD DO DRIVERS DRIVE ON NOW?

18.

Three: Atlantic, Pacific, and Arctic

19.

C. Like a swimmer in cold water, the metal tower is susceptible to temperature-induced shrinkage.

20.

The right. Just before 5:00 a.m. there was a brief country-wide traffic jam as all traffic stopped and switched sides before heading off to start the workday.